I Am What I Say I Am

Felt by: Terryl Lamar Gayden Jr
(named after Terryl Lamar Gayden Sr)

Written by: Lamar Junior (The Artist)

McClure Publishing, Inc.

Copyright © 2024

Terryl Lamar Gayden Jr. for McClure Publishing, Inc.

All rights reserved. Printed and bound in the United States of America. According to the 1976 United States Copyright Act, no part of this book may be reproduced or utilized in any form or by any means, electronic or mechanical, including photocopying, recording, or by any information storage or retrieval system, except by a reviewer who may quote brief passages in a review to be printed in a magazine or newspaper, without permission in writing from the Publisher: Inquiries should be addressed to McClure Publishing, Inc. Permissions Department, 398 West Army Trail Road, Bloomingdale, IL 60108. First Printing: May 30, 2024.

ISBN-13: 979-8-9877802-9-9

Cover Design by Kathy McClure

To order additional copies, please contact:

McClure Publishing, Inc.
https://McClurePublishing.com
800-659-4908

Table of Contents

Page

A Story to Tell	19
The Chapter of Love	21
It Keeps Me Up	23
Love is Love	25
"Love Can Be Hate"	27
Is It Time?	29
Why.. So I can Know	33
Our World	35
Strangers	37
Go Deep	39
Be the One	45
Silence	49
Hope	51
Believe	53
Freedom	55
Grace	57
Never Forget	63
More Than	69
"Art"	71
My Art	73
Tragedy	81
Where Do You Go	93

Be There 95
I Hear You 97
    Biography of Terryl Lamar Gayden Jr

The Philosophy

I kept Lamar because I feel it is the piece of Senior that is there but is not shown. The side of him that I see and at times feel. Junior because I Am Who I Am, Not What I Went Through.

I am a GOAT
I am a CREATOR
I am an ARTIST
I am ART
I am SELF MADE
Epitome of SELF MADE
STAYING POWER
I am a GENIUS
I am GOD'S GIFT

ACKNOWLEDGEMENT

I would like to recognize Amoz Wright.
He took pictures of me that are inside the pages of this book.

THE PURPOSE

Is to let men, Black men, know that it is okay to be vulnerable and have feelings. Expressing those feelings while being vulnerable is also all right. Men, be aware of your emotions and own them. Black men are often taught to hide this side of themselves, even though we are humans, and it is natural. I want this to be a safe place. Your feelings are always valid. It starts with you acknowledging that they exist. You will have to face them and again OWN them. Be "in your feelings," there is nothing wrong with that. Growing up there were times when I was told not to cry by other men. I'm here to tell you, you will be hurt, disappointed, let down or betrayed. You might want to cry but from one man to another, that is okay.

I come from a family where most of the men suppress their feelings. I know I did as a child. Being that I am already introverted, not knowing how to express my feelings properly, as well as not being encouraged to, it was easy for me to suppress my feelings too. This often led me to being passive aggressive and shutting down. Holding things in for so long would lead to outburst. You just get fed up. There are times where I expressed my feelings in the best way I could but there would be roadblocks to lead me back to suppression.

"He's always in his feelings."

"You in yo feelings, acting like a girl."

"You're always complaining."

"He wears his heart on his sleeve."

There's often a misconception within our community that showing or expressing your feelings is "acting like a girl" but only if you express yourself in a nonaggressive way. You don't have to assert your dominance or display signs of anger when your feelings are hurt. Also, another misconception is that expressing your feelings is equivalent to complaining. You are not complaining if your opinion differs from others, or you don't feel the same as everyone and you speak out about it. You are not less of a man when speaking on how you feel and once you understand that you will gain a sense of comfort within yourself. There has to be a level of acceptance on both sides. Within yourself and within our community.

I Am Here to

Innovate : Inspire : Influence

Inform : Inspire : Influence

The Goal

The Goal is to be Successful
The Goal is to be Enlightened
The Goal is to be Happy
The Goal is to retain Peace

The Letter To Myself

Everyone doesn't speak your love language
Friend, Parent, Significant Other
So, you can't expect how you express your love From others
This doesn't mean those dearests to you doesn't show you love
You know they do
You feel it
When You're around
It's been showed
It can be displayed in a multitude of ways
You know when love is not being showed at all
You know hate when you see it
Hear it
You feel that as well
But you've grown
You've gotten away from that
Those that are here are here for good
Here for a reason

There love and support is expressed the best way they know how to express
Or what they've been taught at least continue to spread love
Love will always find its way back to you
But it may not be returned the same way it was given
And you have to accept that
There's only one you
You do things the way you do them
You acknowledge that
You know that
So let people be themselves
You'll know when it's real
But always trust your gut feeling

I Am Who I Am

If you knew the real me
Would you still judge me the way you do
What do you see when you look me in my eyes
What do you hear when you hear my voice
What do you think when you see my braids or my locs
My tattoos
Do you think I'm like the "others"
You put in a box
When you see my dark skin
If you knew the real me
Would you think those same thoughts
Would your perception change or be the same
Are you into assuming

Or would like to take a chance to get to know the real me
Do you deserve to know who I truly am
Well, if your thoughts were far from positive
I rather let you think what you think
I am who I am
And what I been through has never seeped through the clothes that I wear nor tore down the smile on my face
And neither will your misperception of who I am

JBY
("Just Be You")

Does what I write come from a place of hurt or does what I write come from a place of growth?

The scars never go away. Fancy your scars is what they say but I say appreciate them.

Don't cover them, admire them. Look back and be grateful you made it out.

A Story to Tell

I know what it feels like to have family members envious of you and
Jealous of your presence
I know what it looks like to have
Friends jealous of you
Your energy and how people treat you
Soon to Realize they were never there for you
Quick to smile in your face
but spiteful of who you are and your truth
Because they're uncomfortable with themselves
I know what it sounds like to have
People downplay your confidence because they're not confident within
Standing out in a space where you believe in yourself
In front of people who don't
Sounds of people intimidated by your aura
I know what it feels like to talk so much and never be heard
I know what it feels like to lose a loved one but know they're still there... inside
I know feelings of heart break
I know what it feels like to lose someone who never left

I AM WHAT I SAY I AM

I know what it feels like to go through all of this and not let it wear me
nor tear down my sense of self

The Chapter of Love

Love: "an intense feeling of deep affection."

Love: "strong affection for another arising out of kinship or personal ties."

You can be in your feelings and your bag

Come walk with me

It Keeps Me Up

Love keeps me up at night
I don't wanna go to sleep
When you're around
I wanna cuddle with you
I wanna hold you
When I leave
My mind wonders
I want to stay and get to know you
The old you
How you've grown
Have you been hurt
Have you let yourself down
How your parents treated you
I wanna get to know you
I wanna know how you feel
I wanna know how you smell
Are you my type
The amount of kids you would like
What's your favorite color
Are you the materialistic type?
You ever fell in love
Do you feel love will find you again?
Or will you find love?

I AM WHAT I SAY I AM

I wanna meet you
The real you
I wanna get to know you, Love

Love is Love

Love comes in all shapes sizes colors
Different languages
Love has so many different forms
Good and bad
Love can be dark
Love can be hate
Love can be scary
Love is so powerful
Love can change the world
Love should be handled carefully
Love should be easy
But love can be hard
It can be confusing
Afraid to love this being because of their past
Because of your past
Because of your issues
But is this being afraid of love or the lack of
See a new fresh pair of shoes
Oh, I love these
Is that the easy part of love
Or does love not hold much weight
Took me years to fall in love with basketball
Went through a lot of ups and downs
But the love is what keeps me going
Fell in love before but

Love is also letting go
Love has many faces
Love can be shown many ways
Don't love my mother the same way I love my sister
Can't love my sister the same way I love my partner
Sometimes love isn't enough
But sets a very solid foundation
Lead with love
It'll get you far
Everyone deserves love but most important
Everyone should love themselves

"Love Can Be Hate"

Hate is just another form of Love
Why?
Because Hate is only the outcome of the action
Meaning
Hate is only what you put out
The negative energy
Words
Comments
Attitude
But the action itself is Love
The consistency
The obsession
The enjoyment
It only turns into Hate once the "feelings" become negative
The action itself is Love
What you put out is Hate

Is It Time?

When is it too early to say "I love You"

A month, a week, a day, years

Maybe two

How do I know what I'm feeling is love

Is it love or the time I yearned for over these past years

Is it love because I needed that somebody

Or is it you

Can I get this feeling from someone else

Are you feeling what I'm feeling

Do you think this is love too

Or is it too soon

When will too soon pass

When will the phone calls end with

I Love…

Too soon too soon

Ight I'll talk to you later

What About Us?

When you are sharing your space or time and energy with someone there "should" be an energy transfer that allows you to feel loved and understood in a way that makes you feel comfortable.. As well as, allowing you to be yourself.. But it all comes from within. First, you'll bring it out of yourself, and the right person will come along and enhance it and/or add to it. The love you put into yourself and out into the world will come back double.. Love is a language and can be expressed in a plethora of ways.. Teach Love.. Express Love.. Learn Love and Learn From One Another..

Why.. So I can Know

I want us to be abstract
I want us to be unique
In our own way
Your mindset
May differ from the way I think
Your beliefs
Are not parallel with mine
But We build together
To come together
As one
On the basis of understanding
And accepting

We make this
A "foreign exchange".. so to speak
I give to you as you give to me
It's not the norm but it's valuable
Because it's a part of you
It is.. You
And I'm willing to innerstand

I'm willing to learn
With your help
As I'm here to assist with your journey of innerstanding as well
Be my safe place
As I offer a space of comfortability
Our muse
Our differences will not tear us apart
But brings us closer
Simply out of curiosity
Why?
So, I can know
So, I can overstand
The more I ask
The you wonder
The closer we get to one another

Our World

Let's be together and live in our own little world

Away from society's rules

A world where we make the rules

We set the standards

And where our love matters the most

Let me pick your brain

See why you are the way you are

See what got you this far in life

Let's elevate each other

Help each other grow

The beauty of love is what I seek

I hope when we meet, you're as beautiful on the inside as I dream you are on the outside

But is the woman of my dreams

the one I need?

Do I even get enough sleep to find that woman?

Restless nights thinking about whomever

that may be

But at the same time, I think...

Do you ever think about me?

Strangers

I wanna pick your brain

I wanna get inside

Of you

How you think

Why I feel the way I do

When I see you

When I look at you

When I look in your eyes

When we hug

It's more than that

Can we be more than what we are

Why You got trust issues

What happened

Can I know

Are you comfortable

What can I do to make you comfortable

I AM WHAT I SAY I AM

I wanna relax you

Ease your mind

Be your muse

We're in our own world

Just me and you

Can we be more than strangers

Who are you? Where are you?

Go Deep

I want to touch that one spot

I want to go to that one place

That spot inside

The place you let no one go

That place that's hard to get in

Even for you

A place not too many people have been

Not even you

That spot that can lead to something

I want to be that thought that leads to a dream

I want to be your last thought before you close your eyes

Deep down

Let's go there

And connect

Let's be close

I AM WHAT I SAY I AM

And become one

No more dreams

This will be apparent

Sooner than later

I AM WHAT I SAY I AM

For You,

When you look in the mirror, I want you to be able to smile. Not because of how beautiful you look but because of how you feel. Lookin' in the mirror is deeper than what's looking back at you.

Love,

Lamar Junior

Nobody is responsible for Your Triggers

Or Your Feelings

But You're always responsible for how You Treat People

I AM WHAT I SAY I AM

We accept the 10% ... and we can do a lot with it

__Be the One__

Our life is written out before we are born

We are born to be great

Destined to be something

So, take full advantage of your life

You are in control

Don't let others

Control you

Make decisions for you

Sway you

Follow your dreams

Go after what you feel is right

Take risk

Be brave

Stay on track

When you know you know

Sometimes we do fall

I AM WHAT I SAY I AM

We may stumble

But continue on your path

Break those walls

Those barriers

Those curses

I Embrace the dark

because

I am the light

Silence

Emptiness

Maybe even loneliness

Is that what you feel?

When surrounded by silence

Or do you feel a sense of peace?

Don't lose yourself

When in silence

Find yourself

Silence is Golden

Hope

Dreams

We all have them

Our dreams may turn into nightmares

But don't wake up

Push through

There's light on the other side

Don't be afraid

Be confident

Don't be reluctant

Be courageous

It's your time

Have faith

Have ... **Hope**

Believe

Believe in yourself

Be who you are

Stay true to you

You are destined to be something great

Block the noise

Embrace the love

Do what you were born to do

You're here for a reason

Have faith

Spread love

And regain hope

No one can stop you

But you

Stay True

Freedom

Let go

Of the outer world

The distractions

The noise

Come back to reality

Separate yourself

From the fake

From the lies

Find yourself

Embrace the silence

The quietness

Find your inner peace

Love can manifest

If you finally

Let Go

Grace

Show Gratitude

Be Humble

But don't let no one

Take away from what you've earned

Don't let anyone talk to you crazy

Respect is earned

But sometimes you gotta take it

Don't wait on handouts

Don't wait on applause

Pat yourself on the back

You put in the work

You Are Who You Are

Be Who You're Meant To Be

Do What You're Meant To Do

Find Yourself

And never lose sight of the Goal

Be Successful

Give yourself flowers but make sure, you water them
Continue to Grow

Black Men and Our Flowers
Don't get enough of them
Whether that be figuratively
Or Receiving flowers
To brighten our mood
Or a sign of gratitude
Black men and our flowers
Flowers are seen as feminine
Well, we need to give more to that side of us
Flowers aren't meant just for those who lay at rest
Or women
But to those that need to rest and be appreciated
Give me my flowers while I'm here
Give us our flowers while we're here
So, we can appreciate them
Flowers are a part of Art
Flowers are beautiful
Flowers mean something
They represent something
You deserve them
I deserve them
We deserve them
But we don't get them enough
Reflects the fact we don't get what we often feel we deserve
We're the change within that
It starts with us
We must give to one another

There are over hundreds of thousands of species of flowers

We all have our own stories
We all have our own trials
Tribulations
Trauma
But we push forward
We grow
We adapt
The rose that grew from the concrete right?
That's us
Some concrete may have been paved differently
But we all grew out to be something special
Continue to water receive and give flowers
In order to blossom

Never Forget

When we fell on the ground as kids

Blood

Dirt

Scratches

The adrenaline rushes

To just pop back up and continue to

Have fun

Because everything will be okay

I will heal

This time is valuable

This moment is everything

Nothing else matters

Not the pain

Not the dirt

The blood

I will be okay

I will heal

Express Yourself

We don't have to mask our feelings

It's okay to express

Express your feelings

We are human beings

It's normal for us to have emotions

Exfoliate Release Unmask

Reveal yourself

Show your true colors

Be an artist

Express yourself

More Than

I am more than a being

I am more than a human

I am out of the ordinary

I'm different

More than what the plain eye can see

Look deep

I am more

So many pieces to put together

My mind alone is an artist

My body is a canvas

I am Art

I'm no artist

When I write

When I create

My mind is at work

My mind alone is an artist

I AM WHAT I SAY I AM

I create

I express

I feel

I am more than what the plain eye can see

You feel me

My energy runs deep

One specimen

Has such a powerful impact

I am more

No plain eye can see

"Art"

Art

Can be depicted in so many ways

Can be heard

Hand crafted

Spoken

Written

Appreciate all forms of art

I love art

Art embodies who I am

My mind

Body

And Soul

So many layers to Who I am

Not only do I create art

With what I say and what I do

What I see and what I think of

But I Am Art. ME

My Art

Picture this

Standing in the rain

The Rain pours down on us

Our hearts are filled with love

As the rain comes pouring down

But what we see what we feel is hearts

Love showers us

Shower me with love

Your love

Connect with me

As we stand here and soak up this moment

Let's Love one another

That would be magical

Hearts falling from the sky

Onto me

Hearts falling from the sky onto us

I AM WHAT I SAY I AM

We feel it inside

Butterflies

This picture is beautiful

This is my art

Shot by: Amoz Wright

Sometimes I wish that night was just a nightmare. Stitched into my hat are the words, "Welcome to my nightmare." I never thought I'd be here today without my big brother. This half-filled heart on my chest is a representation of the emptiness I feel inside knowing I am living without him. The shaded portion represents the family that's still here loving and supporting me. I know he's up there watching over me. I strive to be the best not just for myself but for him because he believed in me more than anyone else did.

Power & Prosperity

Abundance

Insight

Nourishment

We've all experienced things in life that may have caused us a lot of pain. Whether it be physically, emotionally, or mentally. Some of us heal and some don't. Some of us don't know how, the "proper" way at least. So, we cope the best way we can or suppress and pick up on unhealthy ways to "forget about it." But we have the power to get right. Let Go and Let God. Do not worry, put your stress away and leave it to God. Do things that make you happy. The little things like, thinking positive, having hope, having faith, talking to yourself nice and being generous. Flip the script and make sure the ending is happy. 🤍

Tragedy

"An event causing great suffering, destruction, and distress, such as a serious accident, crime, or natural catastrophe." (Oxford Dictionary)

Where would we be without tragedy

Would we be as strong

Would we be as humble

Is tragedy always bad

Is there some Good

What exactly is tragedy

I mean we seem to enjoy it when it's televised

Put on to the big screen

But what if you're playing that leading role

Seems as if there's no ending

No happy one at least

But you're in control

You're the director

The editor

The star

Change the narrative

Make your ending happy

Not all tragedies have a happy ending

But make sure yours do

Ever lost a loved one

and although you know you're making them proud

You have to accept the fact that they won't be there to see you make it

The pain is deep down inside

the hurt you can't see it in my eyes

This smile will remain on my face because it is a reflection of how you made me feel

Cherish those times of Joy. Hold on to them. I was told they don't last forever. But I'll never forget how it made me feel. There was a time when we were Happy. In this moment in time, it draws me back to then and now I am happy again.

Imagine this

Pro debut December 11, 2021

You're up 3:00 or 4:00 in the morning

Crying for 8 hours straight

Because you know no matter how good or bad

You do today, you can't call and tell your brother about it

You also know your opportunities will

Continue to get bigger

Opportunities will continue to get better

But he won't be there

To encourage you

You can't look into the crowd and see his smile

You can't tell him about the move you did

That You got from him

You call your mom

Ma, I don't think I'll ever heal from this

Ma, I don't think this pain will go away

Ma, I'm going to continue to get better

I will continue to grow

Ma, I'm going to make it

But he's not going to be physically here with me

I know pain

But I keep going because I can feel his presence

I will make it

I will continue to make him proud

The hardest things to express
are your intentions

I AM WHAT I SAY I AM

I am a powerful human being

The same way I can build someone up

I can also tear them down

I can help so many

But I can also hurt

Gift and a curse

I have to be careful and aware

I am above nor beneath anyone

I have to acknowledge my faults

I have to acknowledge my ignorance

Powerful but far from perfect

Knowledgeable but sometimes unaware

Confident but at times confused

A caring being with so much heart

Wants to give so much love

But at times doesn't know how

Can be so focused on what not to do

Subconsciously does it

But in a different way

I AM WHAT I SAY I AM

Follows no one

Leads himself

But can be lost at times

Optimism doesn't always seem to be the answer

Reflection can be broken

But the message is crystal clear

Honesty is easy

But it isn't easy to tell

Easy to say nothing

But hard to keep it within

Fall

You get up

Move forward

Don't follow your footprints

Reflection is broken

But the message is crystal clear

Where Do You Go

At times you were saying all the right things

But at the times it mattered the most all the wrong things came out

Being there for those you feel need it

Helping people grow

But the you that they have

You're missing in your life

You grow from within

Self-reflection

Making mistakes

Realizing how you affect people

Healing

Loses as lessons

And you spread that knowledge

Because you've been there, and you had to find yourself

By yourself

I AM WHAT I SAY I AM

Not everybody knew what you went through

But you kept a smile on your face

You were a lender for a shoulder to cry on

Your tears fell

You wiped them yourself

Be There

I have to uplift

Without falling

Uplifting doesn't always involve carrying

Walk along side of me

Hold my hand

Burdens are easy to carry when we're together

Let me take that weight off your shoulder

There's room on mine

Make room for me

I'm here to help

Assist

Watch you grow

As we Grow together

We shall blossom

I've heard

"Life without love

Is a tree without blossom or a fruit"

Our journey never ends

But there's a part of this story

Where we enjoy the fruits of our labor

I Hear You

Hurt people hurt people

Their intentions aren't to hurt

But to express how they feel

Sometimes in not so healthy ways

In a world full of misunderstanding

You seek to make others feel the way you feel

ANY way possible

Words aren't enough at times

Sometimes physicality seems to be the answer

Mentally scarred

But so, misunderstood

Physically is the only reasonable reaction

Hurt people are misunderstood

Hurt people need love

Hurt people don't hurt themselves

Hurt people deserve to be understood

And loved

An apology isn't enough

Actions speak louder than any word there is

Accountability goes a long way

Hurt people have rights

We've all been hurt before

Learn

Grow

Acknowledge

Accept

I don't know what's best for you

I only can advise from experience

What I've learned and what I've seen

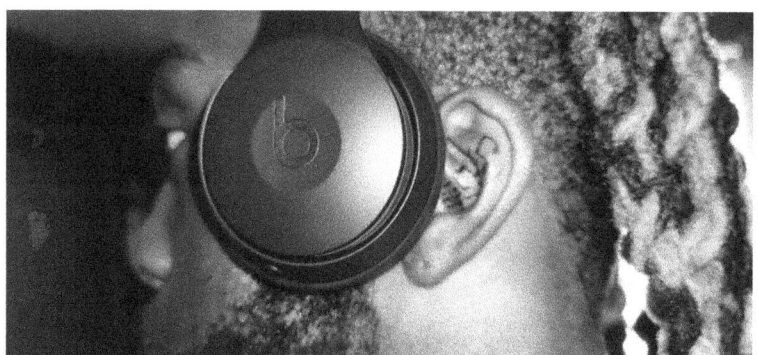

How can you touch me
And it not be physical
You open my mind
Make me think
Deep in my feelings
I hope I don't sink
It's fine if I do
It's just me and you
You don't judge me
Or look at me crazy
I'm really here/hear
For you
To listen
To feel better
when the world is too much
But go on
I'm here for you
To listen
And get the message
You're trying to deliver

INTRODUCTION

A playlist. My playlist. Put together solely by me and based on what makes me feel good. Music now speaks through me. Majority of the music I listen to I can relate to, in more ways than one. So, when you listen to this playlist, I am there with you. Don't just think it reminds you of me. Think, the more you listen the closer you are getting to me. I am walking to the room you are in. The Original name of the playlist was paranormal. Think about paranormal activity but not in a scary way. I am there with you while not being there. You get It. I am letting you into my life. Into who I am. This is Me. What I've been through. What I think. What I want to express but cannot. Some songs take me back to a certain time, place, moment, etc... It is really spiritual.

It comforts me and makes me feel better. The playlist will never be complete. There are songs that were left out because of how I was feeling in that moment. Right now, I am still growing as a man and human being. Which means more songs will be added as time goes on. Maybe when my time has come you all will continue to add to the playlist. These are not just my favorite songs; They're ups and downs. The love. The Pain. The Success. The heartbreaks. The Betrayal, etc. THIS IS ME. Music is Me. I am Music.

*Terryl Lamar Gayden Jr
through
Music*

The Intro About Nothing,

I would like to start by saying it is not Easy Being Me. I can't compare struggles. My struggle is my struggle. Everything was not easy for me growing up. Nothing was handed to me. I worked for and earned everything I have received in my life. I have been told; "If I was you, I would have been stopped." But I Can't Be Broken, and I will keep striving for greatness. I was destined to be great.

God Took His Time with me and my mother always told me to be the best I can be. Many times, I have failed, fallen, many times I have been DEVASTATED but losses are lessons. I have been left with a Heavy Heart. I have cried some nights. Times I have felt alone and Lonely. But in all reality, I have *Sum 2 Prove*, not to anyone but to myself.

I always knew Better Days were ahead and that I will be Legendary. So, until then my Ambition is through the roof. There are No Days Off. Rest is needed but when you are not working physically, work mentally. Plan what's next. Dream big. Work on yourself. Meditate. Study film. Listen to something inspiring or knowledgeable. No days off is not just about physically working.

There is always that Demon in the back of your mind. The doubt. The What If. That's just distractions to deter your focus. I have my close friends that support, show me love, and make sure I am focused. We all have goals and aspirations, so I do the same for them. We Gon Make It, we all will be Successful in our respective careers.

I do feel as if I am the black sheep out of the group. I do feel Misunderstood. I do feel like I do not always get the love and support I give. I am man enough to say that. I don't want to harp on that though or go On & On because I am thankful for the love and support I do receive. I have to tell myself sometimes love is shown in many ways, and I will not always receive the love I give because there is only one me. At the same time, Don't Hold Your Applause for me.

Okay, Okay, let's switch to a more positive light. Although my pain is Expensive Pain, I Praise God and thank him for leading the way. For being by my side through my highs and my lows. I Walk by faith. God will never give me more than I can handle. I may not understand that at the moment, but I know it is for the better. So, when I get through the storm, the rain, the struggle, and the uncertainty, it'll be so much more worth it because I Earned It. Idk why it has to be that way, but I do not complain, I am forever grateful for my journey. God works in mysterious ways.

I manifest, I focus on my goals, and I work hard. My 2020 Vision came to life. 2021 was better than 2020. So, I know that God is always protecting me and aware of my work. I know God Breathed on me. I know there will be times where I may have doubt but when those times come, I put it in God's hands. Once I put it in God's hands, I know I Let it All Work Out. With that being said, I know I always have to hold myself accountable and fulfill my end of the bargain. I can't expect God to Have Me while just doing nothing. I can't be like Here's Whatever and expect big things to happen. I know there is always somebody next or ahead of me. It's either Me or You. And I'm Wit It, whatever you with, x10. I have

Cold Blood when I lock in. Instilled in me by my mother. I was inspired by the greats, Kobe, Mike, AI, etc....

I have had Faygo Dreams since I was a child and have been chasing that dream ever since. It is not a game. I won't allow myself to Think It's A Game. If I miss out on an opportunity it is because I did not put in enough work, or it was not meant for me. I am going to take something from it. I can't blame anybody but myself, it is not the D'Evils work, it was me not putting in enough work. What is meant for me, will be. Once I tapped in, dug deep within, and became closer to God, myself, and one with the universe. We are now Having Our Way. I cannot lose. I want New Balances and abundance. I want people to know my Name Ring Bells around the world.

I have this quote, "The goal is to have a household name outside of your household." I want people in Seattle, Maine, Canada, Africa to know about me. I have played ball in many different areas, states, and countries. There have been times where I was in a bar, scrunched up in a crowd and out of nowhere some random person taps me on my shoulder or noticed me because I was playing basketball somewhere. That is when I knew this was for me and now I will continue to work and get those types of moments on a larger scale. My heart and soul are embedded into this; therefore, I will do nothing less than prevail. My blood, sweat and tears, my passion, my ambition, the hard work I send all that energy up. In return the Universe and God protects and guides me, sounds like a Fair Trade to me.

I AM WHAT I SAY I AM

Learning how to lose is within the process of winning
Losses are a part of the journey
The lesson within the loss is the gem
The diamond in the rough

The upkeep of yourself
Is always in motion
Never ending cycle

Just make sure we don't hang our dreams on a shelf
Stealth training but the impact was loud as can be

Turning my back on myself was to see those who left
That path can be lonely

Following footsteps of your deity
Seeing things from his POV
Shocked that there's light that you see

The reflection of me
Peace
A balanced harmony

A calling
When you answer and realize you're sanctioned to do what's needed
While figuring out what the need is

The need to Innovate
The need to inform

Without the perceived formal wear
Because my best attire
Is my heart that I wear on my sleeve

I AM WHAT I SAY I AM

Come as you are
And I refuse to leave
And not look like me

The need to influence
The need to inspire
Those who's path has seem to take a toll
Well, I have changed
Enough for you and me
I have what it takes to set us free
Of the shackles that have been put on me
And You
Cliché right
But freedom in this world is something we have yet to see
Let's us be
We've come too far
To not be free
But what's free
Because this cost me a lot
Not my new car
But the new scar
And that runs deep
Past the white meat
Expensive Pain
But only talking about it is cheap

Those dearest to Terryl is not solely who this book is for. Not just the close friends and family members. This was orchestrated for anyone who has struggled getting out of their bed. The ones who been at a point where they struggled to put their best foot forward. For those who have been doubted and overlooked. We've all been on the "right' path and stumbled on a brick or two. From one Black man to all those across the globe, we must stick together.

Our people should be our number one priority. Always being asked, "How do you go through life without drugs?" This is part of that way of life and maintaining peace. The writing began in college, and it was simply an expression of feelings that were turned in as assignments.

There was a professor who saw something in Terryl that he did not see in himself. Years went by of his second oldest sister telling him that he should write and publish his own poetry book.

True story, one of Terryl's professors broke down in tears reading a paper he wrote analyzing one of Kobe's interviews. Rest in Peace Kobe Bryant, he was still alive at the time but has always and still is a big influence on and off the court. With that being said, those people saw "IT" before he did and now we're all here. That gratitude and appreciation will be forever. This here is to take a step back from Terryl the hooper. Because being in Mexico playing ball, wasn't what it sounds like, but he remained resilient and continued to be an influence on those around and also the youth. That was always a part of the bigger picture. Being two thousand miles away from home but still being able to touch people with his words and wisdom, only pushed the vision further.

This gives you insight on the influential aspect of being fly and influential. Prospering on this here earth, with the longing to live forever; Lamar is here to inform, innovate, inspire, and influence people.

As one of his favorite artists would say, I Love You, Like you Love Me. Peace 🖤

Biography of Terryl Lamar Gayden Jr

I was born in Argo, Illinois, a lesser-known town nestled just outside of Chicago. Argo holds a unique distinction—it's the birthplace of Emmett Till. A recent sculpture erected in honor of his mother graces the grounds of Argo Community High School.

Barbershop conversations once revealed that the legendary Bernie Mac frequented our neighborhood. My family and I moved around a bit, but the bulk of my formative years unfolded in Dixmoor, Illinois. Third grade marked my arrival there, and it was during this time that I forged lasting friendships, now akin to family bonds.

Education was my unwavering pursuit. From elementary school through high school, I consistently earned a spot on the honor roll. My academic journey led me to Thornton Township High School in Harvey, Illinois, where I graduated in the top 10 of my class. Later, I obtained my bachelor's degree from Saint Xavier University.

Art, Sports, and Music: My Passions

Art captivates me in all its myriad forms—fashion, drawings, paintings, poetry, and cinema. Each creation leaves me in a state of awe, appreciating the human spirit's boundless expression.

While basketball remains a perennial favorite, I've also developed a keen interest in boxing and battle rap. Yes, battle rap—a complex arena where words collide, references abound, and metaphors weave intricate patterns. In college, battle rap and philosophical musings rewired my brain, fostering focus, patience, and understanding. Some battles stretch for hours, demanding attentive listening as opposing wordsmiths spar.

Music, too, occupies a cherished place in my heart. The composition of songs, the arrangement of albums—it all fascinates me. There are moments when I listen and think, "I wish I'd penned those lyrics." One of my aspirations is to craft and share my own song.

Beyond these passions, my hobbies include working out, savoring music, and indulging in a few video games. Life's symphony, composed of diverse interests, continues to unfold.

I love putting together outfits from my closet, creating unique looks. Cooking and grocery shopping allow me to explore flavors and experiment in the kitchen.

www.ingramcontent.com/pod-product-compliance
Lightning Source LLC
LaVergne TN
LVHW061554070526
838199LV00077B/7038